I'd Like to be Like That

LET'S GO DISCOVERY

I'd Like to be Like That

John Marshall

Scripture Union

Scripture Union, 207–209 Queensway, Bletchley, Milton Keynes,
MK2 2EB, England.

ISBN 1 85999 216 1

British Library Cataloguing-in-Publication Data.
A catalogue record of this book is available from the British Library.

Printed and bound in Great Britain by Cox and Wyman Ltd, Reading,
Berkshire.

Contents

*This book is dedicated to all my friends
in the Missions Department of Scripture Union*

Many thanks to:

- Elaine for patiently typing and retyping the manuscript
- Elrose for such creative editing

Chapter one

To be like Barney

Barney sat on a broad bench and enjoyed the warmth of the big bright sun in the brilliant blue sky. He wiped his forehead and closed his eyes. He had been working in his field since early morning.

Barney's real name was Barnabas. We don't know if he ever met Jesus when he was on earth. But we do know that he was one of the first people to believe in Jesus and to follow him. Barney was a good man and full of God's Holy Spirit.

He may have been with all the other frightened followers of Jesus in the upstairs room of a house in Jerusalem at Pentecost when God's Holy Spirit first changed them into daring disciples. That happened just ten days after Jesus had gone back to heaven. We know that he was in the city very soon afterwards, and here he was, sitting in the sun.

Early that morning Barney had walked out from his home in Jerusalem to his field and had been working ever since. He had spent the first half of the day planting cucumbers between the rows of grapevines. Later he hoped to look after the patch where the wheat was growing... but it was a really hot day. He just had to sit down for ten minutes.

Barney wasn't born in Jerusalem. He grew up on the island of Cyprus, hundreds of miles away. Some of his family still lived on the island.

When he first arrived in the city of Jerusalem he had used the money he brought with him to buy his field.

As he sat there with his eyes closed he didn't see Peter coming along the track. Peter saw Barney though and came over.

He gave Barney quite a shock as he sat down next to him. Quickly Barney opened his eyes.

"Peter, it's you! You made me jump," he said.

Peter laughed.

Peter had been a fisherman when the Lord Jesus dared him to work for God. Peter had been with the Lord Jesus when he loved and healed and helped and taught so many people. Peter had seen the Lord Jesus die on the cross. Peter was one of the first people to meet the risen Lord Jesus when he came back from the dead. Peter was now a leader of the church in the city of Jerusalem.

Although Peter laughed when Barney jumped, he didn't smile for long.

"You look worried Peter," Barney said.

Peter sighed and explained, "Since God's Holy Spirit started our church at Pentecost thousands of people have become Christians. It's exciting but at the same time it means that I'm so busy I can't fish any longer. Other leaders can't go out to work either. And on top of that some of our new Christians need help. We need money for food and clothes and homes and families. None of us have got the time to earn it."

Barney thought to himself, I would really like to help but what can I do?

"I'm sorry, Peter," he said, "I wish I had some money to give you to clothe and feed these people. I wish I could help buy homes... but you see I spent all my money on this field."

Peter looked around at the wheat and cucumbers and grapevines. "You've worked hard on this land and it looks good. Well done," he said to Barney.

"Wait a minute, Peter," Barney shouted. He looked as if a big idea was growing in his head. "Things have changed since I became a follower of Jesus. Perhaps I don't need this field as much as other people need houses."

"What?" Peter said. He looked puzzled.

"I'll sell my land!" Barney was nodding. "You can have the money to use for clothes and food and homes and families." Peter knew that the field would be worth lots of money.

"Are you sure, Barney?" he asked. "It's a lot of money to give away... but it would help us enormously."

The very next day Barney went to the market square in Jerusalem and let everybody know that his field was for sale. It wasn't long before he sold it for a large purse of silver coins. Just as he had promised, he gave all the money to Peter and the other church leaders. They were very grateful.

God gave Barney the strength to be a person who shared and cared for others, and particularly helped those in need. God's Holy Spirit was changing the way Barney thought about things. Other people were now more important than some of the things he owned. Much later in the Bible story Barney is described as, "a good man full of the Holy Spirit and faith."

I don't know about you – but I'd like to be like him.

How can we share and care for others?

If we ask him, God's Holy Spirit will help us too.

WORD  GAMES

"Barney sat on a broad bench and enjoyed the warmth of the big, bright sun in the brilliant blue sky."

When so many words in the same sentence begin with the same letter it is called

ALLITERATION   (a-lit-er-ay-shun)

* Try to write a sentence like this about yourself. Here's my attempt.

"John spilt jam and jelly on his jacket so he wore a jade jumper instead."

You might find a dictionary helpful.

* Now try to do the same with a sentence about someone in a Bible story, or even our Great God himself.

BIBLE SEARCH

Do you know what the name Barnabas means?
Look up:

Acts 4:36–37 to find out.

Chapter two

Steve

Steve stood still and silently listened. He knew things were serious by the faces of everyone in the court. He knew things were serious because the magistrate kept calling him by his full name. "Stephen, you stand accused by these witnesses. What do you say?"

When he was growing up Steve would know when his mother was cross with him. "Stephen," she would say, using his full name.

And now the magistrate did the same. "Stephen, can you explain to this court all that has happened recently in our city of Jerusalem?"

His head began to spin with ideas. Should he explain how the leaders of the church had asked him to organise food for some of the hungry? They had seen that Steve was full of faith and the Holy Spirit. He was just the man for the job and he did it really well.

Should he explain how God had given him power to do wonderful things, but that had caused trouble with the members of the synagogue? (A synagogue is the building in which Jews worship.)

Should he explain how he was arrested after people told lies to the temple police – and the same people had just repeated those lies in court?

Steve stood still and looked around the court. None of these thoughts seemed the right thing to say. Then he realised. He had God's good news and he should share it with all these people. He was a messenger – just like an angel. His face shone as he knew what he should say. Everyone needed to know about Jesus.

Everyone was staring at him as Steve started to speak.

He had been through some hard times in his life, but this had to be the most difficult. He really needed God's Spirit to be with him.

As he started Steve reminded everyone how, long ago, God had been with Abraham in the hard times...

then with Joseph in the hard times...

and with Moses in the hard times...

and most recently with Jesus when he had

died on the cross.

Steve thought about all he had learned from Jesus and the disciples in Jerusalem. He looked around at the court. There was anger on lots of faces. People didn't like to hear what he was saying.

Steve was finishing his explanation. "Then you had Jesus killed," he said.

At this everyone in the court seemed furious. Steve stood still in the middle of all the noise and anger. This time he didn't look around at faces. He looked up. Strangely it was as if heaven opened for a moment and he glimpsed the Lord Jesus.

"I can see into heaven," he said, "and Jesus is right next to God."

The people didn't want to hear another word. They rushed at Steve. They grabbed him. They dragged him out of the courtroom. They dragged him down the road and through the city gate. They picked up huge rocks from the hillside. They were furious. They threw the rocks at him.

They stoned Stephen.

Steve stood still. He knew he was dying. His mind flashed back to the day that Jesus died on the cross. That was just outside the city of Jerusalem too. It was as if Steve was suffering, just like Jesus did. He remembered the prayers Jesus had prayed in that hardest of times. Steve always tried to copy Jesus. Now he used his prayers.

"Lord Jesus, receive my spirit," he said.

"Lord forgive these people," he cried as he was knocked to his knees.

Steve died. Steve lay still as if he was sleeping. He went to be with the Lord Jesus in heaven.

Steve was the first person to die because of his faith in Jesus. Since then, millions have died for their faith. We use the word martyr to describe such people. Steve was the first Christian martyr.

We may not have to face death – but there will be hard times in our lives. When problems came, Steve wanted to be like Jesus. He was full of faith and the Holy Spirit.

I don't know about you – but I'd like to be like him.

How can we become more and more like Jesus?

If we ask him, God's Holy Spirit will help us too.

WORD GAMES

Another name for opposites is ANTONYM
(an – toe – nim)

>The antonym of good is bad
>The antonym of large is small

Can you think of the antonym for these words?

ABSENT   PRESENT
BEAUTIFUL   UGLY
CHEAP   EXPENSIVE
FIRST   last
EARLY   Late
OLD   NEW

Sometimes the Bible uses antonyms to show how God's Holy Spirit can help us.

Paul says when I know I'm *WEAK* I can be
STRONG

(2 Corinthians 12:10)

John says: Jesus must become *MORE IMPORTANT*. I must become LESS IMPORTANT
(John 3:30)

Jesus said that everyone who believed in him will *LIVE* even though they DIE
(John 11:25)

That was true of Stephen.

BIBLE SEARCH

Here's where the story of Steve (Stephen) can be found.

Why not look it up. You'll find it in:

Acts 6:8 – 7:60.

And see who looked after the clothes of the people who killed Stephen in Acts 7:58. We'll hear more about him later.

Chapter three

Phil the Unflappable

Phil never fussed or flapped or fretted. He wasn't made that way. "Whenever there's a job to do, however hard, I just get on and do it," he would say. And what he did was always good.

Phil lived in Jerusalem at the same time as Steve.

"Would you be prepared to help Steve distribute food to some needy people in our church?" the leaders asked him. "We believe God has chosen you for this work."

"Of course, I'd love to," Phil replied. "Steve's one of my best friends."

Phil hadn't fussed or flapped or fretted even when the work was hard.

Phil was frightened when Steve was arrested and then killed.

"Jerusalem is becoming such a dangerous place for the friends of Jesus," he said to a friend who could see he was upset.

"I hear that guards are going from house to house looking for us," his friend replied.

"We can't hide much longer," Phil said. "It will be safer if we leave the city."

Phil hadn't fussed or flapped or fretted. Quietly he left Jerusalem. He asked God to show him where he should go. God's Holy Spirit led him to a city in Samaria about twenty-five miles north of Jerusalem. As he went from place to place he started telling people about Jesus.

"I know this is a strange place for me to come to," Phil said to a man, "because my people, the Jews, and your people, the Samaritans have been enemies for hundreds of years."

"You need to be incredibly brave to come here," the man replied. "Why have you come?"

Phil didn't flap. He simply said, "I want to tell everyone about Jesus."

People started to listen. At first it was a few. Two here... three there... and it wasn't long before people crowded around Phil as he explained the good news. He prayed for sick people in the name of Jesus and they got better.

"My dad was lame, but now he can walk," shouted a boy to his neighbour.

Those who were controlled by evil spirits were set free. The city got so excited. There was so much noise in the streets. But Phil didn't fuss or flap. He just enjoyed seeing God at work.

"I wonder what Simon will think," the neighbour whispered.

Simon had lived in the city for a long time. An evil spirit had lived in him for a long time. He had strange powers. Everybody knew him. The rich people thought him amazing. The poorer people just crowded around him. They all wanted to see his evil magic tricks. Simon convinced himself that he was somebody great.

Now everyone was leaving him and crowding around Phil instead. "I must discover more about this person," Simon decided. "His power seems greater than my magic."

Simon went into the city, just to find Phil. Phil had heard about Simon – and now here he was. Phil didn't fuss or flap or fret. He wasn't made that way. He just talked about King Jesus, and then helped people in his name.

Simon marvelled at the miracles. He had never seen anything like it. He saw lots of people in the city believing in Jesus. He started to believe too. He saw lots of people being baptised with water. He copied them. "I want to do the same sort of miracles that Phil does. I want that power," he shouted.

News of all that was happening in Samaria reached the church leaders in Jerusalem.

"We must go and visit," said Peter and John, two of the leaders.

Phil didn't fuss or flap or fret as he welcomed his friends, and heard more about the trouble back in Jerusalem. Peter and John put their hands on the new believers' heads to pray for them – and God's Spirit filled all of them.

Simon had never seen this sort of power before. He held up a purse bulging with silver coins.

"I've earned lots of money with my powers," he shouted. "I will pay you well for this gift. Give me powerful hands like yours."

Peter frowned and stared straight back at Simon. "You cannot buy God's gifts. God knows all about you. May he forgive you for what you are suggesting."

"Please pray for me," Simon said.

Phil didn't fuss or flap or fret as he prayed with Simon. Everyone in the city wanted to spend time listening to Phil. The number of people in the church was growing really fast. Just as God had told Phil to go to Samaria he now told him to leave.

"I want you to leave the big city and go off into the desert," he said.

It's hot and dry and lonely in the desert, Phil

thought. Will I meet anyone there? he wondered.

But Phil didn't fuss or flap or fret. He just followed where God was leading. That's the way he was made. Whenever there was a job to do, however hard, he just got on and did it. And what he did was always good.

I don't know about you, but I'd like to be like him.

If we ask him, God's Holy Spirit will help us too.

WORD GAMES

When Phil was in Samaria people became Christians – and a church was started. A group of Christians makes a church – with or without a building. The real meaning of church is not a building but people. The word church is a GROUP NAME for all the Christians.

Do you know the GROUP NAME for these? (The first one is done to help you!)

A **bunch** of grapes
A _flock_ of birds
A _herd_ of cows
A _bunch_ of flowers
A _bag_ of sweets

See how many other group names you can think of.

BIBLE SEARCH

This part of the story of Phil (Philip) is found in Acts 8:1–25.

Don't read any further or you will know what happens to The Count of Ethiopia!

Chapter four

The Count of Ethiopia

Every day Candace, the Queen Mother of Ethiopia, checked her money. She watched as the court treasurer counted all her gold and riches.

"All this wealth is mine," she smiled, "and you are so good at looking after it," she said to the treasurer. "Whatever shall I do whilst you're away?" The nickname that the Queen Mother had given to her treasurer showed how important he was. She actually called him "The Count", because that's what he did every day. Now everyone in the royal palace called him that (unless, of course, you were a chariot driver, in which case you called him "sir").

The Queen Mother was concerned because she would not have The Count's help for a few weeks. He was off on a journey. She watched as The Count clambered into the chariot and called a command: "TO JERUSALEM!"

"Yes sir," the driver replied.

Ever since his family had arrived in Africa, The Count had wanted to pay one special visit to Jerusalem. He had heard so much about the special religious festivals. He just wanted to go and worship in the temple. But it was a long way to travel. He liked living in Africa. Ethiopia was a fine country, but he wanted to worship the one true God back home in Jerusalem.

The Count had got permission from Candace. She had even given him one of her chariots, as the journey was hundreds of miles. The Count would be away for many weeks.

"Please hurry back," Candace said, as the chariot pulled out of the gateway. "Don't forget to collect all the news," she added. The Count nodded from the back of the chariot.

The stay in Jerusalem was exciting. The Count saw all the city. He worshipped in the temple. It seemed that all the news he heard was about the followers of someone called Jesus. They were claiming that he was the promised Saviour, the Messiah that all Jews were waiting for God to send.

The Count was not looking forward to the long journey home. He had discovered that the chariot was not the most comfortable way to travel long distances. Besides, the scenery was boring – especially the bit through the empty desert to the town of Gaza.

The Count had an idea. He had money. He could buy one of the expensive scrolls on which the Scriptures were written, and read it on the way home. In the palace he could read it to Candace. He chose the part written by the prophet Isaiah. As he carried it to the chariot he knew that the journey home would be more exciting.

The Count climbed into the chariot and called the command: "TO ETHIOPIA."

"Yes sir," replied the driver.

He settled down to read. He decided that each day he would roll open the scroll and read some of it. Then he would try to understand the meaning. After a few days he reached the desert road to Gaza. They were making good time on their journey home.

Today he was reading all about a sheep or a lamb that was killed, and as it died it stayed silent. It was difficult to understand. The Count wondered if it might make more sense if he read it out loud. He tried. It was still too difficult. Suddenly The Count realised that a man was running alongside the chariot. The man called out. "Do you understand what you've just read aloud?"

"How can I unless someone can explain it?"

The Count replied. Then he added, "Can you help?" The man nodded. By now he was so out-of-puff he couldn't speak.

The Count called out a command to the charioteer: "STOP!"

"Yes sir," said the driver, reining in the horse.

"What's your name?" asked The Count.

"Phil," the man replied.

"Come and sit next to me, and explain everything," The Count said. Phil didn't fuss or flap or fret as he clambered into the chariot. The Count called out another command; "TO ETHIOPIA!"

"Yes sir," said the driver. All this stopping and starting was annoying.

"How did you know I would be here?" The Count asked Phil.

"An angel told me to be here. Let me explain that passage you were reading." Phil told The Count that the sheep mentioned wasn't an animal but a way of describing Jesus. "We used to sacrifice lambs but now we don't need to because Jesus has died for us."

Phil took a long time to show The Count all the good news. The Count thought it was all wonderful.

"God must have sent you here for me," he said. After a while The Count saw some water. "Will you baptise me here?" he asked.

"Of course," said Phil.

The Count called out a command: "STOP!"

'Yes sir," said the driver, thinking, "Not again. We'll never get home at this rate."

Phil baptised The Count.

"Come with me back to Ethiopia," The Count said to Phil.

"I can't. God has other plans for me."

The Count watched as Phil disappeared. Then he clambered into the chariot, still wet and called out, "TO ETHIOPIA!"

"Yes sir," the driver said, hoping he could now get some speed up.

The Count was really excited. He had so much to tell Candace. He had so much to read to her. He picked up the scroll again. This is greater treasure than all her gold and jewels, he thought. He read some more. It all began to make sense. God's Holy Spirit was helping him to understand even the hard bits of the Bible.

I don't know about you − but I'd like to be like that.

How can we read and really understand what the Bible is saying?

If we ask him, God's Holy Spirit will help us too. And we can ask older Christians to help explain it to us.

WORD GAMES

Here's a word search on the two stories of Philip. Try to find these words:

CANDACE	JOHN
CHARIOT	PETER
COUNT	PHILIP
ETHIOPIA	SIMON
SAMARIA	

E	T	H	I	O	P	I	A
S	T	H	E	P	C	B	T
I	A	O	O	E	O	K	O
M	O	M	J	T	U	F	I
O	I	O	A	E	N	S	R
N	H	A	I	R	T	A	A
N	P	H	I	L	I	P	H
H	E	C	A	D	N	A	C

If you write out all the letters that have not been used in the answers – you will find the name of the part of the Bible The Count was reading.

E_THE book of isaiah

THE BOOK OF ISAIAH

BIBLE SEARCH

The story of how the man from Ethiopia met Philip is in Acts 8:26–40. When you read it check to see if my story is correct!

Chapter five

The Anonymous Mr A

Mr A wanted to stay that way.
It's not always easy to be a Christian. Mr A
knew that he would have to be brave.
Sometimes it's best to avoid the people who
make trouble. He had just heard that in
Jerusalem the rulers of the temple had started to
attack Christians. Although he lived in
Damascus, a long way from Jerusalem, his town
could be next. If their enemies knew that his
real name was Ananias he would be one of the
first to be arrested.

Mr A heard that Stephen had been
murdered in Jerusalem — just for being a
Christian. They're even killing us now, he
thought.

Worse still, there were rumours that some of

the temple guard led by a man named Saul were heading for Damascus. They had letters giving them permission to hunt down the Christians in the city. It would be better if the Christians hid and used secret names to protect their lives. Mr A wanted to stay that way.

Mr A started to pray.
In these hard times, Mr A thought, it's great to know Jesus is alive and listening to our prayers.

He did not know that, as the soldiers were rushing to Damascus, the Lord Jesus had spoken to Saul through a dazzling light. Saul was now in the same city as Mr A, but he had changed. He believed the same about Jesus as Mr A.

As Mr A was praying Jesus spoke to him in a vision. He told him to go to Judas' house on Straight Street. "Ask for Saul..."

Mr A began to sweat. "But Lord is that *the* Saul who wants us all in prison?" he asked.

Jesus told Mr A that Saul was blind and he had been told that through someone called Ananias he would be given his sight back. "He even knows my name," gasped Mr A.

Jesus said, "I have chosen Saul. He will tell many people about me. He too will suffer because he follows me."

Mr A didn't know what to say.
Mr A knew it would be very hard to do what Jesus was asking of him. He would need to be

very brave. God sometimes asks his people to
do difficult things for him.

Mr A had to obey.
If Jesus asked Mr A to do something he would
surely give his Holy Spirit to help him.

Mr A knew the way.
Straight Street was part of Roman Road, just
past the Market Square. Judas' house was fourth
on the left.

Mr A took a deep breath as he went through
the front door. "Hello!" he shouted.

"In here," a man's voice replied, rather
weakly. "I've been expecting you. You must be
Ananias. Jesus told me in a vision that he would
send you."

"And you must be Saul." Mr A was
beginning to discover that everything was as
Jesus had said. He need not fear Saul.

"Well umm... brother Saul, the Lord Jesus
has sent me. You will see again and receive his
power from his Holy Spirit."

Mr A began to pray.
He placed his hands on Saul's head. As he did,
Saul's sight came back. Saul smiled at Mr A.
Then he shouted, "I CAN SEE! I can see you,
Ananias. I CAN SEE!"

Mr A did not delay.
He found some water. As a sign of his new faith,

Ananias baptised Saul. They had something to eat. Having a meal together is a great way to make friends.

Saul did not delay either. It wasn't long before he was telling everyone how wrong he had been and how Jesus really is the Son of God.

God gave Mr A a difficult job to do. God's Holy Spirit helped him.

I don't know about you – but I'd like to be like him.

How can we be strong when doing a difficult job is the right thing?

If we ask him, God's Holy Spirit will help us too.

WORD GAMES

Isn't it amazing what RHYMES with the letter "A"?

* Can you find some of the words used in the story that rhyme with A?

   Here are some clues to start you off –

   S T--, P--, S--, O---, W--, D-----

   If you need another clue, look at the sentences in heavy print.

* What letter does your name start with? Can you think of some words that RHYME with it?

* Most songs are poetry, put to music. What is your favourite worship song? Why not make up your own worship song?

BIBLE SEARCH

The story of Saul becoming a Christian and
Mr A (Ananias) visiting him is in Acts 9:1–15.
Can you find out how long Saul was blind
before Ananias came to see him?

Chapter six

Joppa Dee

In Joppa, whatever needed doing, Dee would do it.

"You can't set sail without warm clothes," Dee explained to a traveller. "I'll make you some."

Dee lived in the seaside town of Joppa, about forty miles from Jerusalem. The best road was through the town of Lydda (twelve miles away) and on past the groves of trees growing Jaffa oranges. (Jaffa is another name for Joppa.)

"You will need a good thick cloak to wrap out the storms," Dee explained.

There were lots of people using the road because Joppa had a good harbour. It was a busy seaport. Boats were coming and going all the time.

"I'm hoping to sail to Cyprus then on to Turkey and Greece," the traveller said. "It will take a long time."

"Then you'll need the best clothes," Dee had commented.

In Joppa, whatever needed doing, Dee would do it. She was always rushing around, jumping into action to help people. Her friends even called her a gazelle – after the small dainty graceful antelopes that could be seen in the fields between Joppa and Lydda. Those that spoke Aramaic called her Tabitha; those that spoke Greek called her Dorcas. Both words mean gazelle. Some of the children in the church couldn't manage the name Dorcas, so they shortened it to Dee.

Dee was well known for doing good and helping the poor. If anyone was ill, she was there to help.

"Jaffa oranges will give you strength," she said.

If anyone was hungry Dee was there with a basket of food.

"Jaffa oranges for an appetite," she explained.

If anyone was lonely Dee was there for company. Whatever needed doing, Dee would do it.

But Dee was really well-known for her sewing. She was absolutely brilliant. If anyone needed a new robe or cloak or dress, Dee was the person to ask. Everyone wanted to wear the clothing she made as it was the best in Joppa.

Today, though, she was finding sewing difficult. She didn't feel at all well. At first she thought it was just excitement. The traveller had told some exciting stories.

"One of the church leaders, Peter, is at Lydda – only twelve miles away. I was with him last night," he explained.

The story he went on to tell was incredible.

"A man called Aeneas had been unable to walk for eight years. He was lame. Peter told him to walk, 'in the name of Jesus' and he did. It's true. I saw it all."

Dee wanted to know more. She wanted to see for herself.

As the morning wore on Dee felt worse. She had to lie down. She started to feel uncomfortably hot. Her head started to swim. Her mind blacked out. Her friends began to get very worried. Dee died that same day. Everyone was shocked and stunned. Nobody wanted to believe it.

Because Palestine is a hot country funerals take place as quickly as possible. Her friends planned to bury Dee the next day in a cave-like tomb just outside the town walls. Her body was laid in an upstairs room overnight. The house filled up with people crying.

One of the followers of Jesus had an idea. He whispered it to his friend. Together they nodded. "We'll have to be quick though, because Dee's body is due to be buried tomorrow," he said.

They ran the twelve miles from Joppa to Lydda as fast as they could. It wasn't difficult to find Peter. He had a huge crowd of people round him. They explained who Dee was, and what they wanted.

"Please come. We need you. But don't delay. Can you come now?" they asked. "She's going to be buried tomorrow."

Peter thought for a moment. "Yes," he agreed.

All three had never travelled so fast. On the journey the friends told Peter about Dee and her wonderful sewing.

They got to Joppa late that night. The home was still full of sobbing. "Here's some of the clothing Dee has made," said one of the men, pointing to a pile of coats.

"All this reminds me of when I went with Jesus to Jairus" house." Peter thought. He had seen Jesus bring the temple leader's twelve-year-old daughter back from the dead. "And by his Holy Spirit we can still have his power." Then he asked himself, "What did Jesus do?" He decided to do the same.

Peter sent all the wailing women out of the

room, just as Jesus had done. Then he prayed to God. He spoke to the dead person, just as Jesus had done. "What had Jesus said? Oh yes," he remembered.

"Tabitha, get up."

Peter took her hand. (Jesus had done that.)

Dee opened her eyes, saw Peter and sat up. As Peter helped her to her feet she said, "I was coming to see you!"

Peter called everyone back into the room. Now there was lots more crying – but this time with excitement. There was lots of hugging too. One of the believers was a leather worker called Simon. He went up to Peter and said, "You must be tired. Come back and stay at my house."

Dee saw them going and said, "What about some food first? I'll get some."

Someone said, "I expect it will be Jaffa oranges." Everyone laughed. In Joppa whatever needed doing, Dee would do it.

I don't know about you – but I'd like to be like that.

How can we always do good and help the poor?

If we ask him, God's Holy Spirit will help us too.

WORD  GAMES

Can you fit these words from the story into the JIGALINK puzzle?

PETER   SHIRTS   JOPPA

COATS   POOR   SAD

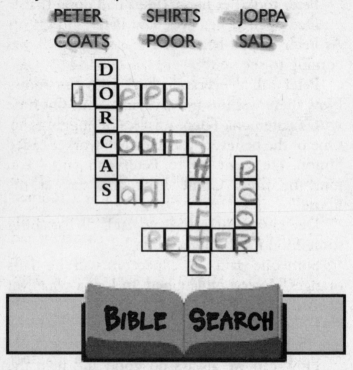

BIBLE SEARCH

Let's take a look in the book. The story of Dee (Dorcas) is in:

Acts 9:36–43.

Can you find the verse that talks about Dorcas "always doing good and helping the poor"?

Chapter seven

Captain Cornelius

Captain Cornelius commanded his soldiers in the seaside city of Caesarea. He was a Roman soldier. When his men saw him in his uniform, his polished helmet glinting in the sun, they had no choice. They had to obey him.

"Alex. I want you to take these two servants and go to the town of Joppa," Captain Cornelius ordered.

The soldier standing in front of him saluted. He didn't dare ask why, but Captain Cornelius went on to explain. "Each day I pray to God."

"Yes sir," the soldier said. Everyone in Caesarea knew that. The city had many temples where different idols and gods were worshipped. The city was even named after the Emperor Caesar, who was worshipped there.

Ever since he had arrived from Italy, Captain Cornelius wanted to discover the one true God. He and his family did all they could to learn of him.

"Today, as I was praying," Captain Cornelius said, "God sent a shining angel in a vision. He told me that there's a man called Peter staying in Simon's house at Joppa. God has a message for me. Peter will tell me what it is. But I must send for him. That's your job, soldier. Take these two servants and go as quickly as you can. If you follow the coast road south, you should be able to get to Joppa by lunchtime tomorrow."

The journey was about 35 miles.

"Yes sir," replied Alex the soldier. Captain Cornelius commanded up to one hundred soldiers in Caesarea. Like Alex, they all had to obey him.

"Excuse me sir," the soldier asked. "How will I find Simon's house?"

"It's somewhere by the sea." Captain Cornelius said. "He makes leather. I'm sure the awful smell of tanning will lead you to the house."

Captain Cornelius thought and added, "I have chosen you, Alex, because I know that you fear God too. Now go as quickly as you can."

Captain Cornelius commanded his soldiers. They had to obey him. But now God was giving the orders, and Captain Cornelius had to obey him. There were some things he just could not do for himself.

Captain Cornelius called for more of his soldiers and commanded them. "Go and invite my friends and relatives to a special meeting at my house. Tell them that in four days we will hear a message from God. They should not miss it."

"Yes sir," the soldiers said. They saluted and left to do just as Captain Cornelius had commanded.

The Captain was right about the time it would take. Around lunchtime the next day Alex reached Joppa and soon found Simon's house down by the sea. What a strong smell, he thought. He stopped by the gate and called out. "Hello there. Is a man called Peter staying here?"

"Hold on, I'm coming down," shouted a voice. A man ran downstairs from the roof. "It's me you're looking for. I'm Peter," he said, puffing a little. "Why have you come?"

The soldier was pleased Captain Cornelius had told him the story. He explained it to Peter.

Immediately Peter said, "I'll come," then he thought and added, "but we can't start back now. It's too far and you need some rest. We'll go tomorrow. Come into the house."

Some of Peter's friends thought, he can't go with them. They're not Jewish. They're foreigners.

The next day Peter and Alex set out with the servants and some of Peter's friends. They were still puzzled but Peter was very keen to go. Eventually Alex asked the question that was on everyone's mind: "Peter, you seemed to expect us when we arrived yesterday. How do you know what's happening?"

It was going to be a long journey to Caesarea which was just as well, because Peter's answer took a while.

"Yesterday I was on the roof of Simon's house, praying," he explained. "It was just before you arrived, just before lunch and I was hungry. God showed me a whole load of animals all trapped in a net. I could see that they were the types of animal I had never eaten. I've always obeyed the Jewish law which won't allow that sort of animal to be used as food. A voice told me to kill them for meat and eat."

"I was shocked. 'No Lord – I can't eat those. They're unclean,' I said. God told me never to say anything is wrong if he says it's right."

"Are you sure that's what you saw?" Alex asked.

"Oh yes. It happened three times," Peter said. "Just as I was trying to work out what it meant you arrived. I was even told in the vision that you were looking for me – and I should go with you."

"How amazing!" said one of the servants

sent by Cornelius.

"I'm sure God is telling me that the good news of Jesus is for everyone, not just the Jews." Peter explained. "Before yesterday I'd always thought of anyone who is not a Jew as unclean."

"And that would include Captain Cornelius," Alex said.

It took two days to reach Caesarea. It was a big city with a large harbour. Peter was glad that Alex led the way to the Captain's house. When Peter walked in, Captain Cornelius rushed over and bowed down in front of him, so low his face touched the ground as he knelt on the floor. The soldier was shocked. He'd never seen the captain do this before to anyone.

"Please stand up," said Peter. "I'm only a man."

"But you have God's message for us," said Captain Cornelius. "Come and meet my family and friends."

When Peter went into the main living room he found it packed with people. There were so many people wanting to hear God's good news. After Captain Cornelius had explained the vision he had had four days ago, Peter began to speak. He told everyone about the Lord Jesus.

"God doesn't have favourites. He sent his son Jesus to die for everyone – but he didn't stay dead. God raised him to life again." Peter looked around. Everyone was listening closely. "Everyone who believes in Jesus will be forgiven. Anybody can believe in him."

The large crowd knew that Peter's message was special. It was from God. His Holy Spirit was there in the room. He was working in them. They all began to praise God. They all wanted to be baptised. Peter ordered that it should happen.

"Please stay with us," Captain Cornelius said.

Peter agreed. "Well, just for a few days," he said.

Captain Cornelius commanded a soldier to sort out the bed rolls in the spare bedroom. "Yes sir," the soldier said. He had to obey.

Captain Cornelius was so used to giving orders, but he knew when he needed to ask for help. He knew he had to take orders from God – however important he thought he was. He knew he had lots to learn from Peter, and he was brave enough to ask for help.

I don't know about you – but I'd like to be like that.

If we ask him, God's Holy Spirit will help us too.

WORD GAMES

The Roman Army didn't really use the title of Captain. Cornelius was called a centurion. He commanded 100 soldiers, and the Latin word "centi" means 100.

Can you fill in these gaps (the first one is done)

- There are 100 years in a: CENTURY

- There are 100 of these in a metre: C M

- There are 100 of these in a US dollar (money): CENT

- This insect is supposed to have 100 legs: Centip

- In cricket when a batsman scores 100 runs it is called a: CENTURY

How old do you think a CENTENARIAN is? 100 YO

In which years will each person in your family be a Centenarian?

BIBLE SEARCH

The story of Cornelius takes up the whole of Acts chapter 10. Make sure you've got a few minutes as it will take a while to read.

Can you spot the name for someone who makes leather? It's in verse 6 and again in verse 32.

Chapter eight

Barney (again)

Barney sat on a broad bench and enjoyed the warmth of the big bright sun in the brilliant blue sky. Following Jesus seemed to be a new adventure every day.

His mind went back to when he had sold his field. "That was a long time ago now," he thought. He looked around him. Jerusalem was such a big city with so many big things to do. "But we've got a big God," he said to himself.

Paul came down the road, saw Barney and walked over. He sat down next to Barney.

"You look worried, Paul," Barney said.

Paul explained. "It's over a year now since I started following the Lord Jesus. You remember when my name was changed from Saul, don't you? Yet still people don't trust me. They think

I'm lying. They think it's a trick. I know in the past I've bullied some of your friends – and that must be difficult to forgive. But I have changed. Yet nobody in the church wants to be my friend." Sadly, Paul looked down at his feet.

"I trust you," said Barney.

"Do you really?" Paul asked, looking up.

"Yes, and I'll be your friend," offered Barney.

"Will you?" Paul could not believe what he was hearing.

"And I'll help you meet all my friends," Barney smiled.

Barney's real name was Barnabas. It means, "someone who encourages others".

"Thank you, thank you. You're living up to your name," Paul said very excitedly.

"Come on, let's start now," said Barney grabbing Paul's arm and pulling him off the seat and in the direction of Peter's house. "Leave all the talking to me. I'll speak for you," he added.

Over the next few weeks Paul proved he really had changed. In fact even the enemies of Jesus could see it and tried to kill him. His new friends smuggled him out of Jerusalem and suggested he went to his home in Tarsus for a while.

★ ★ ★

Barney sat on a broad bench and enjoyed the warmth of the big bright sun in the brilliant blue sky. Following Jesus seemed to be a new adventure every day. It had been a long journey of over 300 miles from Jerusalem north to Antioch. Although it was a large city Barney had found the house church quite easily. They don't have to stay in hiding here, like we have to in Jerusalem, he thought to himself.

A stranger sat down next to him. Barney smiled and said, "I've just come from the church in Jerusalem."

"That's amazing. It's great to welcome you. Have you really travelled all that way just to meet us?" the stranger asked.

Barney nodded. "We've heard about your new church. So many people are coming along. I've come to see for myself."

"That's marvellous," the man from Antioch said. "We are just beginning to discover how good God is – and now you're here. What do you think of us?"

"I'm very excited... and I want you all to keep following Jesus. He really is great."

It was now the stranger's turn to smile. "Thank you," he said. He was no longer a stranger. Now he seemed more like a brother.

Over the next few days Barney got to know more about Antioch. The city had a huge theatre. The enormous arches of the aquaduct bringing water into the city were incredible. He discovered lots more about the new church.

When he met the leaders, Barney said, "You've made a great start, but you do need some help."

They nodded. They knew he was right.

Barney had an idea. "When I leave here," he said, "I'm going to travel up the coast to Tarsus. My friend Paul lives there. I'm going to bring him back here to Antioch with me. We'll become part of this new church. We'll tell you what we know about Jesus and you can tell us what you have discovered. We will need to stay for quite some time. I suggest at least a year."

And that's what happened. For a whole year Paul and Barney taught in Antioch. Huge numbers of people came to hear them. The people of Antioch started to use a new word to describe the believers – Christians. At first it was a joke, a kind of nickname, but everyone in the church was happy to be named after Christ.

The church eventually sent Barney and Paul back to Jerusalem with some money to help the Christians there. "Use this money to buy food. There's going to be a famine," one of the leaders said as they left. "Come back soon and tell us all the news," shouted someone else.

★ ★ ★

Barney sat on a broad bench and enjoyed the big bright sun in the brilliant blue sky. Following Jesus seemed to be a new adventure every day. He had been back in Antioch for some time.

Everyone was pleased to see Paul and him again. They were keen to hear all the news.

Simeon sat down next to him. Simeon was another leader and teacher in the church.

"God has clearly shown us that we mustn't keep the good news about Jesus to ourselves," said Simeon. "It's exciting that Paul and you are willing to share it in other places. Thank you for letting us pray with you before you leave us."

Barney grinned.

Simeon asked, "Have you thought where you might go first?"

"Well," said Barney rubbing his chin, "we thought we would catch a boat and sail over to the island of Cyprus. It's my home country so I know lots of people there... and I really want to tell them all about Jesus."

"Home's a hard place to start," said Simeon.

"It's where I'd like to go first." Barney was serious. "I need to share the good news with my friends and family – then we hope to go to lots of other towns and cities."

And that's what he did. God gave Barney the strength to encourage many people. You see Barney was a good man, full of the Holy Spirit and faith.

I don't know about you – but I'd like to be like him.

If we ask him, God's Holy Spirit will help us share too.

That wasn't the end of Barney's exciting life.

In Cyprus Paul and Barney met an evil, false teacher and a Roman Governor.

In Turkey they were caught up in a riot at another city called Antioch. Their enemies tried to kill them in Iconium.

They were mistaken for gods in Lystra.

In each town they saw people trust Jesus and become Christians.

You see Barney was a good man, full of the Holy Spirit and faith.

I don't know about you – but I'd like to be like him.

WORD GAMES

1 The name Barnabas means "encourager".

Can you guess which meaning fits these people from our stories. Draw a line between the name and the meaning (answers at the end of the book).

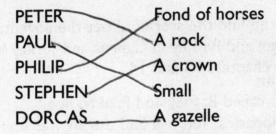

PETER — A rock
PAUL — Small
PHILIP — Fond of horses
STEPHEN — A crown
DORCAS — A gazelle

2 Do you know what your name means? You could find out from a dictionary of first names. My name (John) means a "gift from God".

BIBLE SEARCH

You have to look in three different places to find all of this story.

Start in   Acts 9:26–30
then   Acts 11:19–30
and end at   Acts 13:1–3.

You can find the stories about the adventures of Paul and Barney in Cyprus and Turkey in Acts chapters 13 and 14.

Who called Barney and Paul to be missionaries? You will find the answer in Acts 13:2.

Chapter nine

Timid Tim

Tim was terrified of travel. Whenever people talked about it – he trembled.

"Tim's very timid," his mother would whisper. "He's very shy, you know," she would add.

Tim lived with his mother and father in the small town of Lystra, a lonely place very near the southern mountains in Turkey. That suited Tim. He was scared of anything new. He was terrified of travel.

"Come on Tim. I'm ready to go," his mother called as she adjusted her cloak. She stood by the door of their house.

Tim dragged his heels into the room. Half of him wanted to go... the other half didn't.

"Don't push the boy, Eunice," his father said.

"If he doesn't want to go with you, he can stay here with me."

Tim's mother, Eunice and his grandma, Lois, were going out to a friend's house where all the Christians held their worship. Once he was there Tim enjoyed seeing people. He got on well with everyone. But he also enjoyed his own company. It was hard to leave home, especially when his father stayed back.

"Tim's very timid," Eunice would whisper, and then add, "He's very shy you know."

Tim had learned about God from his mother and his grandma. He couldn't remember a time when he hadn't heard the stories from the Old Testament. He grew up knowing that God really cared for him.

His father didn't believe at all. "I'm a Greek," he would say. "We've got plenty of gods. I don't need another."

"But this is different," Lois would comment. "This really is the truth."

Sometimes Tim just didn't know who to believe.

"Tim wants to come today," Eunice added. "Paul is back in Lystra, and you remember the last time he was here."

Tim's mind went back a few years. That visit was incredible. Since then, nothing as strange had happened in Lystra. Two travellers arrived in the town. It was later discovered that their names were Paul and Barney. The first thing they did was to heal an old lame man who had sat begging in the town centre for years. Tim had seen him by the roadside many times, but always avoided him.

The healing caused a huge stir in the town. Everyone believed that Paul and Barney were gods, come to earth. They wanted to worship them. All Tim's family got caught up in the crowd. Paul stopped the worship when he shouted, "We are not gods. The true God has good news for everyone."

The crowd was now puzzled. Some people started shouting abuse. Others joined in. The crowd turned nasty and attacked Paul and Barney. Tim and his family stood back, shocked as several people tried to kill Paul with stones. They did succeed in dragging him through the town gates and out of Lystra. He was dumped on the dusty road.

Lois and Eunice had followed with Tim. They were among those who helped Paul recover. "That was a close shave," Paul said.

"I think we had better travel on to another town," Barney commented. Tim trembled as he listened. He was terrified of travel.

Paul and Barney secretly came back to Lystra sometime later. "That's when we learnt about Jesus," Eunice would say. "They told us about his time on earth. Paul warned us that things would be hard. That was the start of the church in our town."

Tim had grown a lot in the years since that visit.

"You had better go – or you'll be late," Tim's father grunted. He turned to Tim. "You can stay here if you want to."

Remembering Paul's last visit had made Tim enthusiastic. "I want to go today. I want to hear for myself what Paul has to say."

"Not so keen, my lad," his father said. "Remember you're supposed to be timid!"

Eunice, Lois and Tim got to the house just as Paul began to speak. Tim listened. Paul spoke about Jesus. Everything he had learned from Eunice and Lois began to make sense. "So," Paul said as he finished his talk, "I'm not ashamed of Jesus. I really believe in him."

As he listened Tim had decided he wanted God's Holy Spirit living in him too. As everyone began to go home Tim quietly went up to Paul. "You really are brave to come back," he said. "On your last visit people in this town tried to kill you."

"God's Holy Spirit gives us strength," said Paul.

"People say I'm timid," Tim said, almost thinking out loud.

Paul looked at Tim. "God's Spirit can give you power and love and self-control."

It was all fitting together, "Yes I believe he can," Tim said, surprising even himself with his confidence.

"Then you can be like my son in the faith," Paul laughed.

Over the next few days Paul discovered more about Timothy.

"He's a good lad," said one of the church leaders.

"Eventually he'll make a great leader," said another, quickly adding a cautious, "I think."

A day or two before Paul was due to leave Lystra he met with Tim's family. He wanted to ask a hard question. "Will you let Tim join me in my travels, telling people about Jesus?"

"Oh, Tim's terrified of travelling," his mother said.

"Ask the boy," Lois suggested.

"He can stay here with me, if he wants to," his father added.

Tim had a huge grin on his face. "It will be hard, but I would really love to come," he said slowly. "Thank you."

Paul put his hand on Tim and prayed for him. "Give him your Holy Spirit of power and love," he asked.

Over the next few years Tim travelled to Greece and Jerusalem and Italy; sometimes with Paul; sometimes on special journeys with messages for churches. When Paul was in prison for being a Christian Tim cared for him. At one time in his life Tim was also in prison. Paul chose Tim to be the person to take over from him. Two letters that Paul wrote to him are still part of the New Testament. They are called 1 and 2 Timothy.

God's Holy Spirit changed Tim from being someone who was scared, shy and frightened. He became a leader who was strong and brave.

I don't know about you – but I'd like to be like that.

If we ask him, God's Holy Spirit will help us too.

COURAGEOUS
BOLD
HEROIC
DARING
FEARLESS

WORD GAMES

The words shy and timid mean much the same thing. Words like that are called SYNONYMS, pronounced SIN-O-NIMS. Here are some other synonyms for Timid: Afraid; Nervous; Bashful.

When God's Holy Spirit worked in Tim he made him brave. Some of these words are synonyms for brave. Can you find which ones?

Brittle

Courageous

Cheeky

Bold

Heroic

Frightening

Daring

Fearless

Cunning

BIBLE SEARCH

You can find the stories at Lystra in
Acts 14:8–20
and Acts 16:1–3.

Timothy is mentioned in lots of other Bible
bits. Can you find what Paul called Timothy in
the following verses. The first one is done for
you. (You may need to ask someone to help
you.)

1 1 Corinthians 4:17   My son

2 Romans 16:21   MY FELlOW worker

3 1 Thessalonians 3:2   BROTHER

4 Philippians 1:1   Servant

Chapter ten

To listen like Lydia

Lydia lazily leaned against a lime tree and listened. Once a week she used to leave the huge noisy city of Philippi and walk out into the countryside and down to the river.

"I'm always so busy in the city," she thought to herself. "So many people want to buy my purple cloth. I never seem to have a moment to myself. I do enjoy coming out of the city each week."

Lydia had a secret no one else knew. She knew how to make purple dye from the roots of the madder plants. It gave cloth a beautiful deep colour. Lydia had learnt how to make the dye when she was growing up in the Turkish town of Thyatira. Lydia knew she could sell lots of purple cloth to the rich Romans as they really liked the colour. All the emperors wore purple togas. So she moved hundreds of miles overseas to Philippi, a Roman city.

Lydia's cloth was as popular as she hoped and now she was a rich merchant in the city. She had her own house with many servants to do the cooking, cleaning and gardening.

Ever since Lydia first arrived in Philippi she had wanted to find out all she could about God – not the Roman gods worshipped in the many temples in the city, but the one God that all the Jews spoke about. In most towns there was a synagogue where Lydia could have gone into a courtyard to listen to the teachers.

"Excuse me," she had asked one of her customers, "could you please tell me where the synagogue is in this town?"

The man had shrugged his shoulders. "There's no synagogue in Philippi," he said. "Every Sabbath day the few Jewish worshippers get together in a meadow by the river, just west of the city."

That's why Lydia went there, and lazily leaned against a lime tree to listen.

Except one day was different. There were some visitors. Lydia heard them introduced as Paul and Silas from Antioch.

Paul was speaking. He talked about God in a way that Lydia had never heard before. He explained that someone called Jesus was the promised one, the Messiah for whom all Jews were waiting. "He is called the Christ."

"Because of this, we have been given a new nickname, Christians," Paul explained. Lydia joined in as everyone laughed.

Suddenly though she was very quiet and listening hard.

"Jesus was killed," Paul said, "but wait a moment. The story doesn't end there."

Lydia was amazed as she heard that God raised him to life again and he's still alive.

"Because his death was punishment for the wrong things we have done, we can be forgiven. Because he is still alive we can have a new start in life." Paul's words were wonderful.

This was the good news that Lydia had been wanting to hear. As Paul spoke it all seemed so right. Lydia understood. Her smile grew wider and wider. She had lots of questions about God – and here was someone with answers.

Lydia left the shadow of the lime tree and spoke to Paul as he finished his talk. "I really believe you are right," she said.

Paul and Silas looked at each other. "God has brought us here for Lydia," Silas said. "I knew it was right to come over to Greece."

"Will you come to my home?" Lydia asked. "It's big enough for you to stay there while you're in our city."

Paul and Silas hesitated.

"If we all belong to God, we should be one family," Lydia said.

Paul agreed and they followed Lydia home.

But all that was in the past!

Lydia still leaned against a lime tree and listened. Only now it was in her own garden. Only the rich could afford homes with gardens. Lydia no longer needed to go to the river each week. Now those who believed in Jesus could meet in her house.

Not everything was that easy.

One day Paul and Silas were arrested and taken to the city court. The magistrates ordered them to be whipped and locked in prison.

Some of Lydia's neighbours weren't too happy about having people like that staying in the street.

Paul and Silas could have escaped when God sent an earthquake. Instead they stayed in the cell – and the jailer and his family all became believers. They joined the group of Christians meeting in Lydia's house.

Some of Lydia's neighbours weren't too happy about having both criminals and jailers in their road.

The magistrates asked Paul and Silas to leave the city. Just before that happened they insisted on going back to Lydia's home for one last praise time in the garden.

Some of Lydia's neighbours aren't too happy

about the noise of the singing in their neighbourhood. Lydia no longer leans lazily against the lime tree. Now she's busily following Jesus. Every day she is trying to be the person he wants her to be. Life will never be the same again. It's never been so exciting.

God gave Lydia the strength to be a person who shared her home because she believed. God's Holy Spirit was changing the way Lydia lived. It all happened after God's Holy Spirit opened her mind and made her willing to accept what Paul was saying.

I don't know about you – but I'd like to be like her.

How can our belief grow really strong?

If we ask him, God's Holy Spirit will help us too.

WORD GAMES

Did you notice in the story of Lydia that she

   listened and said

      yes to Jesus. She

         decided to follow him so

            invited Paul to her house. He

            accepted.

Using the letters of LYDIA like this is called an acrostic. Can you make one with your name? Here's mine.

   just

      one

         happy man

         now

Can you make one for Paul or Peter?

BIBLE SEARCH

Lydia's story is found in:

         Acts 16:13–15.

If you want to read about Paul and Silas in the earthquake you'll have to finish the chapter (to verse 40).

Chapter eleven

Cilla

The words drifted out across the whole market place. "Terrific tents mean luxury living."

"Cilla's selling again," said the man on the fruit stall to one of his customers.

"Terrific tents, made like they're meant to be."

Cilla was standing in the front of her shop, in the busy city of Corinth. With her husband she made and sold tents. When customers came she would introduce herself; "Welcome to Aquila and Priscilla's shop, where you will find the best tents in Corinth. We make them ourselves, on the premises. This is my husband, Aquila. Please call me Cilla. All my friends do."

Corinth was a huge city, and there was always need for good tents. These were not for camping holidays, but to live in. Many people in the Greek countryside around about lived in tents. Many of the sailors using the two busy ports nearby needed tents for their travels.

Cilla was beginning to feel at home in Corinth. "It might be a big place," she would say, "but you ought to see Rome, the capital of the Empire."

Cilla and Aquila had lived in Rome until last year. The Emperor Claudius had ordered that all the Jews should be expelled from the city. Cilla and Aquila were forced to leave. "Especially you two," one of the Roman soldiers had shouted as he pointed to them. "The Emperor doesn't want Christians in his capital city."

"But what will my customers do? We make the best tents you know." Cilla had replied.

The people of Corinth had discovered that. The tents sold almost as quickly as they were made.

"That's excellent stitching. The hem is perfect," said the stranger.

"You know something about tents, do you?" asked Cilla, her eyes raised.

"I used to make them, before I started travelling," the stranger replied. Cilla looked interested so the man continued. "With my friends I'm visiting many towns and cities with the message of Jesus. There's not much time for tent making now."

Cilla's heart jumped. "You're followers?" she asked but before the man could answer she said, "So are we. We discovered the Good News in Rome. We've longed to meet other Christians since we've left... but you're the first."

The man introduced himself. "My name is Paul."

Cilla gasped. "Not THE Paul of Tarsus we've heard so much about?" she asked excitedly.

"That's me," the man admitted.

"Please come in. Stay with us. A Q U I L A," Cilla shouted, "you'll never believe who's here... in our shop." She turned to Paul. "Come through to the back. My husband will consider it an honour to meet you. You must be hungry. I'll find some food."

Just at that time Paul needed some friendly faces. Life had been difficult recently.

Paul stayed with Cilla and Aquila all the time he was in Corinth. That was eighteen months. They all became very good friends. Sometimes Paul helped with the tent making, especially if there was an extra large order to finish quickly.

Every weekend Paul spoke to the Jews in the synagogue. Cilla and Aquila went with him. One day some of those listening did not like what they were hearing. Paul had to leave the building in a hurry. The house of another Christian, Titius, was right next door, so Paul went there. The ruler of the synagogue became a Christian. Lots of people followed. There were lots of baptisms.

Cilla and Aquila were excited at how quickly the church was growing.

Other Jews continued to be difficult. Cilla encouraged Paul. "Keep going," she said. "You are doing what's right."

"God has told me to keep on speaking," Paul answered. "He is with us. No one can harm us."

"Aquila and I have been threatened by the Emperor's soldiers in Rome," Cilla said. "We're not going to run away from this lot."

"God has also told me he has many people in this city," Paul replied, "and you are two of the best."

Paul was taken to court. When he was in danger Cilla and Aquila risked their lives for him.

"Paul, we all know that Corinth is dangerous," Cilla would say. "There is so much evil here. People don't like God's message. But you should see Rome. It's even worse. Please be brave enough to take God's message there too."

Cilla and Aquila kept mentioning Rome. Paul thought about it. "One day..." he would say, his words trailing off into more thoughts.

After a year and a half Paul knew it was time to travel on, but not to Rome. He wanted to go to another very important city called Ephesus. It was in Turkey. "I've never been there before, but I've heard so much about the place," Paul said.

"The temple to the false god Artemis is there," Cilla said. "I've heard it is an incredible building."

"Then I must tell them about the true God," Paul said bravely.

"We're coming with you. You'll need good friends," said Cilla and Aquila. "Now that the church here is big, it doesn't need us as much as you do."

It was quite a long sea crossing to Turkey.

As soon as they arrived in Ephesus Cilla and Aquila made a new home. Paul stayed a while but then needed to travel further. Cilla and Aquila settled in their new house. It wasn't long before they were inviting other guests. One weekend the speaker in the synagogue told everyone about Jesus, but he didn't seem to know the whole story. When he finished Cilla spoke to him.

"Apollos, come home with us. We want to tell you the rest of that story."

Apollos became an important Christian teacher and travelled to many churches.

Soon Christians in Ephesus were using Cilla and Aquila's home for their worship meetings. When Paul came back to Ephesus he found a group of people ready to help him.

Some time later Cilla and Aquila moved

back to Rome. It wasn't long before the Christians there were using their home for worship meetings.

Eventually Paul did visit Rome.

Cilla and Aquila quietly got on with their jobs and helped lots of people. Sometimes, when Paul was around, they were hardly noticed, but they were there. They were very important. They were good, reliable friends to lots of people. You could depend on them.

I don't know about you – but I'd like to be like them.

If we ask him, God's Holy Spirit will help us too.

WORD GAMES

I like making word chains – where the last letter of one word becomes the first letter of the next word. Use the clues from the stories in this book to complete this word chain.

1 Cilla's husband

2 Mr A's full name

3 Paul's original name

4 Tim's grandma

5 He was the first Christian martyr (full name)

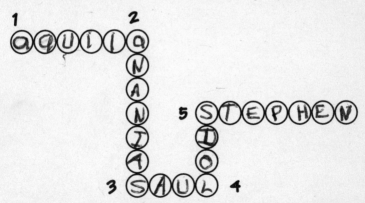

Can you make up another word chain using the names from these stories? Why not start with PHILIP.

BIBLE SEARCH

The story of Priscilla and Aquila is found in Acts chapter 18, especially verses 1–3 then verses 18–26.

Who else was in Corinth with Paul? See verse 5.

P.S.

The Bible is full of people who are now very famous. In the book of Acts we meet Peter, John and Paul as well as Jesus. Most of us have heard their names before.

But there are also lots of ordinary people.

We know the names of some of them: Ananias, Dorcas, Barnabas. We just have to guess others like The Count.

Yet these ordinary people became extra-ordinary people when God's Holy Spirit gave them power and strength. We've discovered some of their stories in this book.

If we ask him, God's Holy Spirit can change us too. He lives in each of us when we invite Jesus into our lives. Each of the people in this book have got special stories because they are

Christians. God wants to do exactly the same for us.

I don't know about you – but I'd like to be like them.

If we ask him, God's Holy Spirit will help us. Here's a prayer you might like to use:

Father God
I know that you take ordinary people
and make them extra-ordinary.
I'm sorry that I so often ignore you.
Thank you that Jesus loves me and died for me.
I open my life to you;
Come in by your Holy Spirit.
Make me the person you want me to be.
Give me the power to follow you. Amen

Answers

1 BARNEY

Bible Search

Barnabas means "an encourager"

2 STEVE

Word Game

Absent	Present
Beautiful	Ugly
Cheap	Expensive
First	Last
Early	Late
Old	New

Bible Search:
   STRONG
   LESS IMPORTANT (or lesser)
   DIE
Saul looked after the clothes.

3 PHIL

A flock of birds
A herd of cows
A bunch (or bouquet) of flowers
A packet of sweets

4 THE COUNT

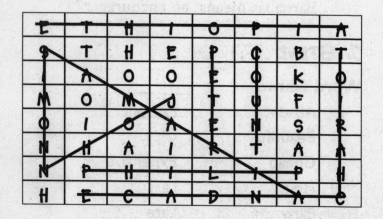

THE BOOK OF ISAIAH

5 The Anonymous Mr A

Word Game

  Stay, pray, say, obey, way, delay

Bible Search

  3 days.

6 Joppa Dee

Word Game

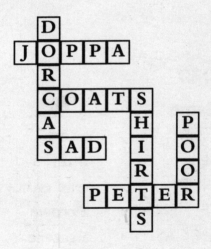

Bible Search

  It's verse 36.

7 CAPTAIN CORNELIUS

Word Game

Centimetre

Cent

Centipede

Century

100 years old

Bible Search

A tanner

8 BARNEY

Word Game

PETER	a rock
PAUL	small
PHILIP	fond of horses
STEPHEN	a crown
DORCAS	a gazelle

Bible Search

The Holy Spirit

9 Timid Tim

Word Game

Courageous

Bold

Heroic

Daring

Fearless

Bible Search

2 My fellow-worker

3 Brother

4 Servant

11 Cilla

Word Game

1 Aquila

2 Ananias

3 Saul

4 Lois

5 Stephen

Bible Search   Silas and Timothy

Other books from Scripture Union

Puzzle Zone
Another excellent **Let's Go** book!

If you enjoy puzzles, then you'll love the **Puzzle Zone**. Let Tara, Jack, Boff and all the other **Let's Go** characters lead you into a world of puzzles...

There are word-searches, picture mazes, spot-the- difference puzzles and quizzes. Each puzzle is based on Bible characters and passages, so you learn about the Bible and have fun at the same time.

Time won't stand still!

ISBN 1 85999 186 6
Price £2.50

The Bicycle Man
Peter Simmonds

If you enjoy adventure stories, don't miss **The Bicycle Man**.

Joel is mad about bikes, especially mountain bikes. When his old BMX is stolen from outside the supermarket his school friends decide to hunt for the criminal. Joel longs to have a new mountain bike. He makes a new friend – Norman Allen, owner of the local bike shop. Norman is building a special mountain bike for Dave, who is trying for a place in the Olympic team. Joel is in for some surprises.

ISBN 1 85999 183 1
Price £3.99

NEW! ROLLER-COASTERS BOOKS

*A great new series of books for 6–8s with lots of
pictures. Roller-coasters are easy and fun to read.*

Bernard Bunting: Worm Doctor
Ro Willoughby

Meet Bernard Bunting and
his friend Brian who decide
to rescue worms in danger of
being squashed. Bernard's pet
worm, String, disappears. So
does the class hamster, Sting,
when Bernard brings it home
one weekend. Will he ever
find String and Sting?

ISBN 1 85999 218 8
Price £3.50

Bernard Bunting: Spider Spotter
Ro Willoughby

Bernard Bunting goes on a camping holiday with his family. He tries to spot a spider or two and keep them. It's more difficult than he first thought.

ISBN 1 85999 217 X
Price £3.50

**Available from Christian bookshops or
SU Mail Order on 01865 716880.**